California DMV

Practice Tests

Prep Book and Practice Questions and Answers for the
California DMV written test

ISBN: 9798385564613

MANCUNIA
PUBLISHING

Book Cover by L. Sweeney

HELLO NEW DRIVERS!

Attention all aspiring drivers in California! Are you ready to take your written driver's test and score higher than you ever thought possible?

This comprehensive guide is designed to provide you with all the knowledge, skills, and confidence you need to ace the written driver's test and pursue your dreams of driving on the roads of California.

Get ready to discover a new level of understanding and mastery of the written driver's test material. Say goodbye to confusion, frustration, and stress, and hello to a confident, stress-free test-taking experience.

Driving is a freedom and a privilege that offers endless opportunities for personal and professional growth. From the moment you start your journey as a driver, you will experience a world of benefits that will shape your life in ways you never imagined. Whether you are looking for the convenience and independence of driving, the chance to explore new places, or a career that requires driving, driving has it all.

One of the biggest benefits of becoming a licensed driver is the convenience and independence it provides. Being able to drive gives you the ability to go where you want, when you want, without having to rely on others for transportation.

Practice Exam

This practice exam consists of the most commonly tested questions in preparation for the California DMV Driving Test. It will typically take about 25 to 45 minutes to complete all questions within the test. The DMV written test is a crucial step toward obtaining your instruction permit. If you are under 18, you need to correctly answer 38 out of 46 questions, achieving an 83% passing score. However, for individuals over 18, the test consists of only 36 questions, but still requires a passing score of 83%. The examples provided in this guide consist of 36 questions.

You will not be allowed any materials on the test day so you should refrain from looking things up in this book or through other sources if you're trying to get a true reflection of how you might do in the real test.

Once you've completed the test identify the areas which you need to revise and then attempt the test for a second time. If you do reach the pass mark you should still continue revising the areas that you didn't do as well in.

PRACTICE TEST 1

Question 1: You may park your vehicle on a sidewalk:

Option A: Only to pick up or drop off passengers

Option B: At any time, as long as the sidewalk is clear

Option C: Never, it is illegal to park on a sidewalk

Option D: During the daytime, but not at night

Question 2: What is the proper hand signal for making a right turn in California?

Option A: Left arm extended straight out the window

Option B: Left arm extended upward

Option C: Right arm extended straight out the window

Option D: Right arm extended upward

Question 3: What should you do if you approach a traffic signal that is flashing yellow?

Option A: Stop and wait for the signal to turn green

Option B: Slow down and proceed with caution

Option C: Speed up to make it through the intersection before the signal turns red

Option D: Ignore the signal and proceed as normal

Question 4: What is the minimum age requirement to obtain a Class C driver license in California?

Option A: 15 years old
Option B: 16 years old
Option C: 17 years old
Option D: 18 years old

Question 5: What should you do if you are involved in a minor traffic collision and there are no injuries?

Option A: Leave the scene immediately
Option B: Exchange information with the other driver and call the police
Option C: Wait for the police to arrive and file a report
Option D: Call your insurance company and leave before the police arrive

Question 6: If you are driving and a fire truck, ambulance, or police vehicle approaches you with its sirens on, you should:

Option A: Speed up to get out of the way
Option B: Pull to the right and stop
Option C: Ignore the siren and continue driving
Option D: Pull to the left and stop

Question 7: What is the proper hand signal for making a left turn in California?

Option A: Right arm extended straight out the window

Option B: Right arm extended upward

Option C: Left arm extended straight out the window

Option D: Left arm extended upward

Question 8: What should you do when you see a pedestrian crossing the street at a marked crosswalk?

Option A: Ignore the pedestrian and proceed as normal

Option B: Yield the right-of-way to the pedestrian

Option C: Speed up to get through the crosswalk before the pedestrian

Option D: Sound your horn to warn the pedestrian

Question 9: What is the minimum age requirement to obtain a provisional license in California?

Option A: 14 years old

Option B: 15 years old

Option C: 16 years old

Option D: 17 years old

Question 10: What should you do if you are involved in a collision and your vehicle is blocking the flow of traffic?

Option A: Leave your vehicle where it is and walk away from the scene

Option B: Move your vehicle to the side of the road, if possible

Option C: Wait for the police to arrive and leave your vehicle where it is

Option D: Drive your vehicle away from the scene, if possible

Question 11: You should always wear a seat belt:

Option A: Only when you are driving on the highway

Option B: Only when you are driving in the city

Option C: Only when you are driving in rural areas

Option D: At all times while driving or riding in a vehicle

Question 12: What should you do when you approach a roundabout in California?

Option A: Stop and wait for all vehicles to clear the roundabout

Option B: Yield the right-of-way to any vehicle already in the roundabout

Option C: Drive as fast as you can through the roundabout

Option D: Drive in the right lane and make a right turn at the roundabout

Question 13: What should you do when you approach a traffic signal that is showing a steady yellow light?

Option A: Stop and wait for the signal to turn green

Option B: Speed up to make it through the intersection before the signal turns red

Option C: Slow down and proceed with caution

Option D: Ignore the signal and proceed as normal

Question 14: What is the minimum age requirement to obtain a motorcycle license in California?

Option A: 15 years old

Option B: 16 years old

Option C: 17 years old

Option D: 18 years old

Question 15: What should you do if you are involved in a collision and there are injuries?

Option A: Leave the scene immediately

Option B: Exchange information with the other driver and call the police

Option C: Wait for the police to arrive and file a report

Option D: Call your insurance company and leave before the police arrive

Question 16: What should you do if you approach a flashing red light at an intersection in California?

Option A: Treat it as a stop sign and come to a full stop

Option B: Treat it as a yield sign and proceed with caution

Option C: Ignore the signal and proceed as normal

Option D: Treat it as a green light and proceed with caution

Question 17: If you are driving and come upon a road sign with diagonal stripes, you should:

Option A: Slow down and be prepared to stop
Option B: Ignore the sign and continue driving
Option C: Speed up to get through the area quickly
Option D: Drive around the sign

Question 18: What is the purpose of a double yellow line on the roadway?

Option A: To indicate a passing lane
Option B: To separate lanes of traffic traveling in opposite directions
Option C: To indicate a bicycle lane
Option D: To separate a right-turn only lane from a through lane

Question 19: If you are driving and come upon a road sign with an image of a crossbuck, you should:

Option A: Slow down and be prepared to stop
Option B: Ignore the sign and continue driving
Option C: Speed up to get through the area quickly
Option D: Drive around the sign

Question 20: What should you do if you are involved in a collision and there is no one available to witness the accident?

Option A: Leave the scene immediately

Option B: Exchange information with the other driver and call the police

Option C: Wait for the police to arrive and file a report

Option D: Take a picture of the damage and leave the scene

Question 21: What should you do when you approach a school bus that has stopped to pick up or drop off children in California?

Option A: Pass the bus on the right side

Option B: Pass the bus on the left side

Option C: Stop at least 20 feet from the bus and wait for the children to board or exit

Option D: Ignore the school bus and proceed as normal

Question 22: What should you do when driving behind a slow-moving vehicle?

Option A: Drive closely behind the slow vehicle to pressure them to drive faster.

Option B: Pass the slow vehicle on the right.

Option C: Pass the slow vehicle on the left.

Option D: Wait patiently behind the slow vehicle until it is safe to pass.

Question 23: What should you do if you are driving and encounter a detour or road closure?

Option A: Ignore the detour or road closure and drive through the closed area.
Option B: Make a U-turn at the next available opportunity.
Option C: Follow the detour signs or take an alternate route.
Option D: Stop your vehicle and wait for further instructions.

Question 24: When changing lanes, what should you do before merging with other vehicles?
Option A: Make eye contact with other drivers
Option B: Use your horn
Option C: Turn your signal on and look over your shoulder
Option D: All of the above

Question 25: What should you do if you are involved in a collision and the other driver does not have insurance?

Option A: Leave the scene immediately
Option B: Exchange information with the other driver and call the police
Option C: Wait for the police to arrive and file a report
Option D: Contact your insurance company for assistance

Question 26: What should you do when approaching a parked car with someone inside it?

Option A: Drive closely to the parked car

Option B: Slow down and be prepared to stop

Option C: Drive around the parked car on the right side

Option D: Drive around the parked car on the left side

Question 27: What should you do when driving behind a fire truck or ambulance with flashing lights and sirens?

Option A: Follow the vehicle closely

Option B: Drive around the vehicle quickly

Option C: Pull over to the right and stop

Option D: Speed up to get ahead of the vehicle

Question 28: What is the meaning of a yellow traffic light?

Option A: Stop immediately

Option B: Slow down and proceed with caution

Option C: Increase speed to beat the red light

Option D: Make a U-turn if safe

Question 29: What should you do when approaching a red arrow traffic signal?

Option A: Stop and wait for the signal to turn green

Option B: Slow down and proceed with caution

Option C: Increase speed to beat the red arrow

Option D: Make a U-turn if safe

Question 30: What should you do when approaching a green arrow traffic signal?

Option A: Stop and wait for the signal to turn yellow
Option B: Slow down and proceed with caution
Option C: The driver making the right turn has the right of way
Option D: Make a U-turn if safe

Question 31: What should you do when approaching a four-way stop sign?

Option A: Slow down and proceed with caution
Option B: Stop and wait for the first vehicle to proceed
Option C: Increase speed to beat the other vehicles to the stop sign
Option D: Drive through the stop sign without stopping

Question 32: What is the minimum following distance you should maintain when driving behind a motorcycle?
Option A: 2 seconds
Option B: 3 seconds
Option C: 4 seconds
Option D: 5 seconds

Question 33: What should you do when you are driving on a road with a continuous white line?
Option A: Cross the line to pass other vehicles
Option B: Follow the line and stay in your lane

Option C: Drive on the left side of the road

Option D: Cross the line to change lanes

Question 34: What is the minimum tire tread depth required by law in California?

Option A: 2/32 of an inch

Option B: 4/32 of an inch

Option C: 6/32 of an inch

Option D: 8/32 of an inch

Question 35: What should you do if you are involved in a collision and the other driver is at fault?

Option A: Leave the scene immediately

Option B: Exchange information with the other driver and call the police

Option C: Wait for the police to arrive and file a report

Option D: Contact your insurance company for assistance

Question 36: What is the maximum length of a recreational vehicle that can be driven without a commercial license in California?

Option A: 25 feet

Option B: 35 feet

Option C: 45 feet

Option D: 55 feet

PRACTICE TEST 1: ANSWERS

1. Option C: Never, it is illegal to park on a sidewalk
2. Option D: Right arm extended upward
3. Option B: Slow down and proceed with caution
4. Option B: 16 years old
5. Option B: Exchange information with the other driver and call the police
6. Option B: Pull to the right and stop
7. Option D: Left arm extended upward
8. Option B: Yield the right-of-way to the pedestrian
9. Option C: 16 years old
10. Option B: Move your vehicle to the side of the road, if possible
11. Option D: At all times while driving or riding in a vehicle
12. Option B: Yield the right-of-way to any vehicle already in the roundabout
13. Option C: Slow down and proceed with caution
14. Option D: 18 years old
15. Option B: Exchange information with the other driver and call the police
16. Option A: Treat it as a stop sign and come to a full stop
17. Option A: Slow down and be prepared to stop
18. Option B: To separate lanes of traffic traveling in opposite directions
19. Option A: Slow down and be prepared to stop

20. Option B: Exchange information with the other driver and call the police

21. Option C: Stop at least 20 feet from the bus and wait for the children to board or exit

22. Option D: Wait patiently behind the slow vehicle until it is safe to pass.

23. Option C: Follow the detour signs or take an alternate route.

24. Option D: All of the above

25. Option D: Contact your insurance company for assistance

26. Option B: Slow down and be prepared to stop

27. Option C: Pull over to the right and stop

28. Option C: Proceed with caution

29. Option B: Slow down and proceed with caution

30. Option C: The driver making the right turn has the right of way

31. Option B: Stop and wait for the first vehicle to proceed

32. Option A: 2 seconds

33. Option B: Follow the line and stay in your lane

34. Option A: 2/32 of an inch

35. Option B: Exchange information with the other driver and call the police

36. Option B: 35 feet

PRACTICE TEST 2

Question 1: What is the maximum length of a combination of vehicles that can be driven with a commercial license in California?

Option A: 60 feet
Option B: 70 feet
Option C: 80 feet
Option D: 90 feet

Question 2: What is the minimum insurance coverage required by law in California for a motor vehicle?

Option A: Liability insurance
Option B: Comprehensive insurance
Option C: Collision insurance
Option D: No insurance is required

Question 3: What is the minimum age requirement to obtain a regular driver's license in California?

Option A: 15 years old
Option B: 16 years old
Option C: 18 years old
Option D: 21 years old

Question 4: What should you do if you have a flat tire while driving in California?

Option A: Keep driving until you reach your destination
Option B: Pull over to a safe location and change the tire
Option C: Call for assistance and wait for help to arrive
Option D: Drive on the flat tire and hope it will hold up

Question 5: What should you do if you are approaching a railroad crossing and the warning signals are active?

Option A: Increase your speed and cross the tracks as quickly as possible.
Option B: Stop your vehicle at least 15 feet from the nearest rail.
Option C: Continue through the crossing as long as the way is clear.
Option D: Turn around and take a different route.

Question 6: What is the minimum following distance you should maintain when driving behind another vehicle on a highway?

Option A: 1 car length for every 10 mph
Option B: 2 car lengths for every 10 mph
Option C: 3 car lengths for every 10 mph
Option D: 4 car lengths for every 10 mph

Question 7: What should you do when you approach a stopped school bus with flashing red lights?

Option A: Stop behind the bus
Option B: Pass the bus on the right
Option C: Stop in front of the bus
Option D: Drive around the bus on the leftl

Question 8: If a traffic signal is out of order, you should treat the intersection as:

Option A: A four-way stop
Option B: A yield sign
Option C: A do not enter sign
Option D: A no parking zone

Question 9: What should you do if you experience a sudden change in road conditions while driving in California?

Option A: Slam on the brakes and skid to a stop
Option B: Slow down and adjust your speed and driving accordingly
Option C: Speed up and try to drive through the change in conditions
Option D: Swerve to avoid the change in conditions

Question 10: What should you do when approaching a railroad crossing in California?

Option A: Drive over the tracks as quickly as possible
Option B: Stop and look both ways for trains
Option C: Honk your horn to warn other drivers
Option D: Drive around the crossing

Question 11: If you are driving on a one-way road with multiple lanes, you should:

Option A: Drive in the left lane
Option B: Drive in the center lane
Option C: Drive in the right lane
Option D: Drive in any lane you choose

Question 12: What should you do if you approach a railway crossing with no signals or gates?

Option A: Drive around the crossing
Option B: Stop before reaching the crossing and look both ways
Option C: Speed up to cross the railway crossing quickly
Option D: Honk your horn to warn other drivers

Question 13: What is the minimum age requirement to obtain a commercial driver's license in California?

Option A: 18 years old
Option B: 21 years old
Option C: 25 years old
Option D: 30 years old

Question 14: What should you do if you encounter a school bus with its red lights flashing in California?

Option A: Pass the bus on the right side
Option B: Stop and wait until the bus turns off its red lights
Option C: Drive around the bus on the left side
Option D: Honk your horn to warn the bus driver

Question 15: What should you do when approaching an emergency vehicle with its lights flashing in California?

Option A: Drive faster to get out of the way
Option B: Pull to the right side of the road and stop
Option C: Honk your horn to warn the emergency vehicle
Option D: Drive around the emergency vehicle on the left side

Question 16: When you are driving and encounter a winding road with hills, you should:

Option A: Slow down and use a lower gear
Option B: Speed up to get over the hills quickly
Option C: Drive in the right lane
Option D: Drive in the left lane

Question 17: If you are driving on a highway and approach a car that is disabled on the shoulder, you should:

Option A: Slow down and proceed with caution
Option B: Stop and offer assistance
Option C: Drive around the disabled vehicle

Option D: Ignore the disabled vehicle and continue driving

Question 18: When driving on a highway, you should always stay in the:

Option A: Left lane
Option B: Right lane
Option C: Center lane
Option D: Lane of your choice

Question 19: What should you do if you encounter a vehicle with a flat tire in California?

Option A: Drive around the vehicle as quickly as possible
Option B: Move to the right lane and slow down
Option C: Drive close behind the vehicle to push it off the road
Option D: Honk your horn to warn the driver

Question 20: When is it illegal to use your cell phone while driving?

Option A: When driving in a school zone
Option B: When driving on a divided highway
Option C: When driving at any time
Option D: When driving in heavy traffic

Question 21: When is it legal to drive in the carpool lane in California?

Option A: When driving alone
Option B: When carpooling with two or more people
Option C: When carpooling with three or more people
Option D: When carpooling with four or more people

Question 22: What is the minimum amount of liability insurance required in California?

Option A: $10,000
Option B: $15,000
Option C: $25,000
Option D: $50,000

Question 23: What is the maximum number of passengers allowed in a carpool lane during non-peak hours?

Option A: 2 people
Option B: 3 people
Option C: 4 people
Option D: 5 people

Question 24: When driving on a wet road, what should you do to maintain control of your vehicle?

Option A: Drive faster to get through the wet area quickly
Option B: Drive the same speed as in dry conditions
Option C: Reduce speed and increase following distance
Option D: Increase speed and decrease following distance

Question 25: What is the minimum speed limit on a two-lane road unless otherwise posted?

Option A: 40 mph
Option B: 50 mph
Option C: 60 mph
Option D: 70 mph

Question 26: What is the maximum number of days you have to renew your driver's license in California after it has expired?

Option A: 30 days
Option B: 60 days
Option C: 90 days

Option D: 180 days

Question 27: What is the maximum number of passengers a new driver under the age of 18 is allowed to have in the car while driving with a provisional license in California?

Option A: One passenger
Option B: Two passengers
Option C: Three passengers
Option D: No restrictions

Question 28: What is the minimum speed limit on a residential street in California?

Option A: 25 miles per hour
Option B: 20 miles per hour
Option C: 35 miles per hour
Option D: 15 miles per hour

Question 29: What should you do if you encounter a road crew working on the highway in California?

Option A: Drive around the road crew as quickly as possible
Option B: Move over one lane if possible and slow down
Option C: Honk your horn to warn the road crew
Option D: Drive close behind the road crew to make them move faster

Question 30: What should you do if your engine stalls while driving on a highway?

Option A: Pull off to the side of the road
Option B: Try to restart the engine while still driving
Option C: Push the car to the side of the road
Option D: Get out of the car and walk away

Question 31: What should you do if you are driving and a vehicle ahead of you is signaling to change lanes?

Option A: Drive in the center of the lane
Option B: Drive around the vehicle quickly
Option C: Slow down and be prepared to stop
Option D: Speed up to prevent the vehicle from changing lanes

Question 32: What should you do when you approach a red light at an intersection in California?

Option A: Stop and wait for the light to turn green
Option B: Proceed through the intersection if the way is clear
Option C: Run the red light if there is no cross traffic
Option D: Turn left even if there is a "No Turn on Red" sign

Question 33: What is the maximum speed limit on a highway with no posted speed limit signs?

Option A: 55 mph
Option B: 60 mph
Option C: 65 mph
Option D: 70 mph

Question 34: What should you do if you encounter a funeral procession on the road in California?

Option A: Drive around the procession as quickly as possible
Option B: Move over one lane if possible and slow down
Option C: Honk your horn to warn the drivers in the procession
Option D: Drive in between vehicles in the procession

Question 35: What should you do when driving in California and approaching a railroad crossing with no warning signals or gates?

Option A: Slow down and look both ways
Option B: Drive across the tracks without stopping
Option C: Stop and wait until a train passes
Option D: Speed up to cross the tracks before a train arrives

Question 36: What should you do if you're driving and a vehicle ahead of you is signaling to make a U-turn?

Option A: Drive around the vehicle quickly
Option B: Drive in the center of the lane
Option C: Slow down and be prepared to stop
Option D: Speed up to get through the intersection first

PRACTICE TEST 2: ANSWERS

1. Option C: 80 feet
2. Option A: Liability insurance
3. Option B: 16 years old
4. Option B: Pull over to a safe location and change the tire
5. Option B: Stop your vehicle at least 15 feet from the nearest rail.
6. Option B: 2 car lengths for every 10 mph
7. Option A: Stop behind the bus
8. Option A: A four-way stop
9. Option B: Slow down and adjust your speed and driving accordingly
10. Option B: Stop and look both ways for trains
11. Option D: Drive in any lane you choose
12. Option B: Stop before reaching the crossing and look both ways.
13. Option B: 21 years old
14. Option B: Stop and wait until the bus turns off its red lights
15. Option B: Pull to the right side of the road and stop
16. Option A: Slow down and use a lower gear
17. Option A: Slow down and proceed with caution
18. Option D: Lane of your choice
19. Option D: Honk your horn to warn the driver
20. Option C: When driving at any time
21. Option B: When carpooling with two or more people

22. Option C: $25,000

23. Option C: 4 people

24. Option C: Reduce speed and increase following distance

25. Option A: 40 mph

26. Option B: 60 days

27. Option A: One passenger

28. Option A: 25 miles per hour

29. Option B: Move over one lane if possible and slow down

30. Option A: Pull off to the side of the road

31. Option C: Slow down and be prepared to stop

32. Option A: Stop and wait for the light to turn green

33. Option D: 70 mph

34. Option B: Move over one lane if possible and slow down

35. Option A: Slow down and look both ways

36. Option C: Slow down and be prepared to stop

PRACTICE TEST 3

Question 1: At what blood alcohol concentration (BAC) are drivers considered legally drunk in California?

Option A: 0.08%
Option B: 0.05%
Option C: 0.10%
Option D: 0.03%

Question 2: What is the minimum distance you must signal before making a turn?

Option A: 100 feet
Option B: 50 feet
Option C: 75 feet
Option D: 25 feet

Question 3: What is the minimum speed limit on a two-lane undivided highway?

Option A: 40 mph
Option B: 55 mph
Option C: 60 mph
Option D: 65 mph

Question 4: What should you do if you are driving on a highway and see an emergency vehicle with flashing lights behind you?

Option A: Pull over to the right side of the road and stop
Option B: Continue driving since the emergency vehicle can pass you
Option C: Speed up to get out of the way of the emergency vehicle
Option D: Slow down and move to the left lane

Question 5: When passing another vehicle, you must return to the right-hand lane when:

Option A: You can see the front of the passed vehicle in your rearview mirror.
Option B: The vehicle you have passed is completely out of sight.
Option C: You are at least one car length ahead of the vehicle you have passed.
Option D: You have safely passed the vehicle and are back in the right-hand lane

Question 6: What is the maximum speed limit for a school bus that is loading or unloading passengers?

Option A: 25 mph
Option B: 30 mph
Option C: 35 mph
Option D: 40 mph

Question 7: What is the minimum following distance for a vehicle traveling at 60 mph or less?

Option A: 1 second
Option B: 2 seconds
Option C: 3 seconds
Option D: 4 seconds

Question 8: When passing a cyclist, what is the minimum safe passing distance required by law?

Option A: 1 foot
Option B: 2 feet
Option C: 3 feet
Option D: 4 feet

Question 9: What is the minimum speed limit for a vehicle traveling on a freeway?

Option A: 45 mph
Option B: 50 mph
Option C: 55 mph
Option D: 60 mph

Question 10: What is the minimum safe following distance for a vehicle traveling at 50 mph or more?

Option A: 2 seconds
Option B: 3 seconds
Option C: 4 seconds
Option D: 5 seconds

Question 11: What is the maximum speed limit for a vehicle traveling on a scenic highway?

Option A: 55 mph
Option B: 60 mph
Option C: 65 mph
Option D: 70 mph

Question 12: When making a right turn, what should you do before turning?

Option A: Check your blind spot
Option B: Signal for at least 100 feet
Option C: Turn on your headlights
Option D: Honk your horn

Question 13: What should you do if a police officer signals for you to pull over?

Option A: Ignore the signal and continue driving

Option B: Slow down and pull to the side of the road when it is safe to do so
Option C: Stop in the middle of the road
Option D: Speed up and try to get away

Question 14: What should you do if your brakes fail while driving?

Option A: Shift into a lower gear
Option B: Use your emergency brake
Option C: Abandon the vehicle
Option D: Apply pressure to the brake pedal

Question 15: What is the penalty for driving under the influence (DUI) of drugs or alcohol in California?

Option A: Fine of up to $1,000
Option B: Imprisonment of up to 6 months
Option C: License suspension of up to 10 years
Option D: All of the above

Question 16: What should you do if you approach a green light that has just turned yellow?

Option A: Speed up to get through the intersection before the light turns red
Option B: Slow down and prepare to stop if necessary
Option C: Proceed through the intersection without stopping
Option D: Stop in the middle of the road

Question 17: What is the minimum distance you must signal before changing lanes?

Option A: 100 feet
Option B: 50 feet
Option C: 25 feet

Option D: 10 feet

Question 18: What should you do when approaching a stop sign?

Option A: Slow down and proceed with caution
Option B: Stop only if other vehicles are present
Option C: Stop only if you see pedestrians
Option D: Roll through the stop sign without stopping

Question 19: What is the maximum speed limit for a vehicle traveling on a mountain road?

Option A: 35 mph
Option B: 40 mph
Option C: 45 mph
Option D: 50 mph

Question 20: What is the maximum blood alcohol concentration (BAC) limit for driving in California?

Option A: 0.10%
Option B: 0.08%
Option C: 0.05%
Option D: 0.01%

Question 21: What should you do if you are being passed by another vehicle?

Option A: Speed up to keep pace with the passing vehicle
Option B: Move to another lane if it is safe to do so
Option C: Slow down to allow the passing vehicle to pass
Option D: Brake suddenly to warn the passing vehicle

Question 22: What should you do if you are approaching a school bus that has stopped to pick up or drop off children?

Option A: Stop and wait for the bus to leave
Option B: Slow down and proceed with caution
Option C: Pass the bus on the left
Option D: Pass the bus on the right

Question 23: What should you do if you are driving and encounter a bicycle in the same lane as you?

Option A: Speed up to get around the bicycle
Option B: Slow down and pass the bicycle carefully
Option C: Honk your horn to warn the bicyclist
Option D: Swerve into another lane to avoid the bicycle

Question 24: What should you do if your vehicle begins to skid on a slippery surface?

Option A: Accelerate and steer in the direction of the skid
Option B: Apply sudden pressure to the brakes
Option C: Steer in the opposite direction of the skid
Option D: Shift into neutral

Question 25: What is the minimum age required to obtain a provisional license in California?

Option A: 16 years old
Option B: 17 years old
Option C: 18 years old
Option D: 19 years old

Question 26: What should you do if you approach a roundabout and there is a vehicle in the roundabout yielding to you?

Option A: Stop and wait for the vehicle to exit the roundabout
Option B: Yield to the vehicle in the roundabout and proceed when it is safe to do so

Option C: Drive aggressively and force your way into the roundabout
Option D: Honk your horn to warn the vehicle in the roundabout

Question 27: What is the maximum speed limit for a vehicle traveling on a California expressway?

Option A: 55 mph
Option B: 60 mph
Option C: 65 mph
Option D: 70 mph

Question 28: How close can you park to a fire hydrant?

Option A: 20 feet
Option B: 10 feet
Option C: 5 feet
Option D: 15 feet

Question 29: From which age can you apply for a Class C driver's license in California?

Option A: 16 years old
Option B: 18 years old
Option C: 15 years old
Option D: 17 years old

Question 30: What is the maximum fine for failing to obey a traffic signal or sign in California?

Option A: $100
Option B: $200
Option C: $300
Option D: $400

Question 31: What should you do if you are driving on a road with a single broken yellow line?

Option A: Drive on the left side of the broken line
Option B: Drive on the right side of the broken line
Option C: Drive on either side of the broken line
Option D: Drive in the middle of the broken line

Question 32: What should you do if you encounter a road sign with a yellow background and black letters?

Option A: Ignore the road sign
Option B: Slow down and proceed with caution
Option C: Stop and wait for further instructions
Option D: Drive around the road sign quickly

Question 33: What is the maximum speed limit for a vehicle traveling on a California highway with no posted speed limit signs?

Option A: 55 mph
Option B: 60 mph
Option C: 65 mph
Option D: 70 mph

Question 34: What should you do if you are involved in a small accident with no injuries to either party?

Option A: Drive away from the scene
Option B: Exchange information with the other driver and file a report with the DMV
Option C: Wait for the police to arrive
Option D: Argue with the other driver

Question 35: What should you do if you encounter a road sign with a white background and black letters?

Option A: Drive around the road sign quickly
Option B: Slow down and proceed with caution
Option C: Ignore the road sign
Option D: Stop and wait for further instructions

Question 36: What is the minimum distance you should leave between your vehicle and the vehicle in front of you on a two-lane road?

Option A: 2 seconds
Option B: 3 seconds
Option C: 4 seconds
Option D: 5 seconds

PRACTICE TEST 3: ANSWERS

1. Option A: 0.08%
2. Option B: 50 feet
3. Option B: 55 mph
4. Option A: Pull over to the right side of the road and stop
5. Option A: You can see the front of the passed vehicle in your rearview mirror.
6. Option A: 25 mph
7. Option B: 2 seconds
8. Option B: 2 feet
9. Option B: 50 mph
10. Option B: 3 seconds
11. Option B: 60 mph
12. Option B: Signal for at least 100 feet
13. Option B: Slow down and pull to the side of the road when it is safe to do so
14. Option B: Use your emergency brake
15. Option D: All of the above
16. Option B: Slow down and prepare to stop if necessary
17. Option A: 100 feet
18. Option A: Slow down and proceed with caution
19. Option D: 50 mph
20. Option B: 0.08%
21. Option C: Slow down to allow the passing vehicle to pass
22. Option A: Stop and wait for the bus to leave
23. Option B: Slow down and pass the bicycle carefully
24. Option C: Steer in the opposite direction of the skid
25. Option A: 16 years old
26. Option B: Yield to the vehicle in the roundabout and proceed when it is safe to do so
27. Option C: 65 mph
28. Option B: 10 feet
29. Option A: 16 years old
30. Option D: $400

31. Option C: Drive on either side of the broken line
32. Option B: Slow down and proceed with caution
33. Option A: 55 mph
34. Option B: Exchange information with the other driver and file a report with the DMV
35. Option B: Slow down and proceed with caution
36. Option A: 2 seconds

PRACTICE TEST 4

Question 1: When making a right turn on a red light, what should you do?

Option A: Stop and look for pedestrians and traffic before proceeding
Option B: Drive through the red light without stopping
Option C: Make a U-turn at the intersection
Option D: Yield to pedestrians and oncoming traffic

Question 2: What is the maximum speed limit for a vehicle traveling on a California residential street with posted speed limit signs?

Option A: 25 mph
Option B: 30 mph
Option C: 35 mph
Option D: 40 mph

Question 3: When should you use your vehicle's turn signals while driving?

Option A: Only when you're driving on the highway
Option B: Only when you're changing lanes
Option C: Only when you're turning at an intersection
Option D: Anytime you're changing direction or moving in a different lane

Question 4: What should you do if you are involved in an accident and there is property damage only?

Option A: Drive away from the scene
Option B: Exchange information with the other driver and file a report with the DMV

Option C: Wait for the police to arrive
Option D: Argue with the other driver

Question 5: What is the maximum number of passengers allowed in a Class C vehicle in California?

Option A: 2
Option B: 4
Option C: 6
Option D: 8

Question 6: What should you do if you encounter a stopped emergency vehicle with its lights flashing on the side of the road?

Option A: Drive past the emergency vehicle without slowing down
Option B: Slow down and move over to the lane farthest from the emergency vehicle
Option C: Stop in the lane closest to the emergency vehicle
Option D: Speed up to get past the emergency vehicle quickly

Question 7: When is it illegal to park your vehicle on a sidewalk?

Option A: At any time
Option B: During the day
Option C: At night
Option D: Only during the rush hour

Question 8: What is the maximum speed limit for a vehicle traveling on a California expressway with no posted speed limit signs?

Option A: 50 mph
Option B: 55 mph
Option C: 60 mph

Option D: 65 mph

Question 9: What should you do if you are involved in an accident and there are injuries?

Option A: Drive away from the scene
Option B: Exchange information with the other driver and file a report with the DMV
Option C: Call 911 and wait for medical and law enforcement assistance
Option D: Argue with the other driver

Question 10: What is the maximum number of passengers allowed in a Class M vehicle in California?

Option A: 2
Option B: 4
Option C: 6
Option D: 8

Question 11: What should you do when approaching a green light that has just turned yellow?

Option A: Increase speed to get through the intersection quickly
Option B: Come to a complete stop
Option C: Proceed with caution
Option D: Speed up and run the light

Question 12: A two-headed arrow with one head pointing straight ahead and the other pointing to the left means that

Option A: You can proceed straight ahead or turn left
Option B: You can turn left
Option C: You can proceed straight ahead or merge left
Option D: You can turn right

Question 13: What is the maximum speed limit in a school zone in California?

Option A: 20 mph
Option B: 25 mph
Option C: 30 mph
Option D: 35 mph

Question 14: What should you do if you are involved in an accident and there is a dispute over who is at fault?

Option A: Argue with the other driver
Option B: Call the police and wait for them to arrive
Option C: Exchange information with the other driver and file a report with the DMV
Option D: Drive away from the scene

Question 15: What should you do if you're driving in heavy rain and your windshield wipers can't keep up?

Option A: Drive faster to get through the rain more quickly
Option B: Pull over to the side of the road and wait for the rain to stop
Option C: Turn off the windshield wipers
Option D: Stop using the windshield wipers and rely on the defrost setting

Question 16: What should you do if you are driving and encounter a construction zone?

Option A: Drive through the construction zone at the same speed as before
Option B: Slow down and follow the posted speed limit in the construction zone
Option C: Drive around the construction zone using the shoulder of the road

Option D: Ignore the construction zone and continue driving at the same speed

Question 17: What should you do if you're driving and a large truck starts tailgating you?

Option A: Speed up to increase the distance between you and the truck
Option B: Brake suddenly to teach the trucker a lesson
Option C: Move to the right lane if it is safe to do so
Option D: Wave the trucker through

Question 18: What should you do if you're driving and a vehicle ahead of you is signaling to make a left turn?

Option A: Drive around the vehicle quickly
Option B: Drive in the center of the lane
Option C: Slow down and be prepared to stop
Option D: Speed up to get through the intersection first

Question 19: What should you do if you are involved in an accident and there is no dispute over who is at fault?

Option A: Argue with the other driver
Option B: Exchange information with the other driver and file a report with the DMV
Option C: Call the police but do not wait for them to arrive
Option D: Drive away from the scene

Question 20: What should you do if you're driving and a vehicle ahead of you is signaling to make a right turn?

Option A: Drive around the vehicle quickly
Option B: Drive in the center of the lane
Option C: Slow down and be prepared to stop
Option D: Speed up to get through the intersection first

Question 21: What should you do if you're driving and a vehicle ahead of you has a broken taillight?

Option A: Drive around the vehicle quickly
Option B: Honk to alert the driver his/her tail light is broken
Option C: Pass the vehicle on the right
Option D: Pass the vehicle on the left

Question 22: What should you do if you are driving and suddenly lose control of your car?

Option A: Slam on the brakes
Option B: Turn the steering wheel in the direction of the skid
Option C: Apply the emergency brake
Option D: Take your foot off the accelerator

Question 23: When driving at night, what should you do when you see a pedestrian walking in your lane?

Option A: Pass quickly
Option B: Honk your horn continuously
Option C: Slow down and be prepared to stop
Option D: Speed up to get around the pedestrian

Question 24: What should you do when changing lanes on a multi-lane road?

Option A: Use your turn signal
Option B: Speed up before changing lanes
Option C: Weave in and out of lanes
Option D: Do not signal when changing lanes

Question 25: What is the maximum number of passengers allowed in a Class B vehicle in California?

Option A: 2
Option B: 4
Option C: 6
Option D: 8

Question 26: What should you do if you approach a stop sign and there is a vehicle in the intersection?

Option A: Stop and wait for the vehicle to clear the intersection
Option B: Drive through the intersection before the other vehicle
Option C: Honk your horn to get the other vehicle to move
Option D: Drive around the other vehicle

Question 27: What should you do when you are passing a bicycle on the road?

Option A: Pass the bicycle quickly to get back in your lane
Option B: Honk your horn to signal the bicycle to get out of your way
Option C: Allow at least three feet of clearance when passing the bicycle
Option D: Drive close to the bicycle to make it move faster

Question 28: What should you do if you are driving in the left lane and a faster vehicle approaches from behind?

Option A: Speed up to block the faster vehicle
Option B: Move to the right lane to allow the faster vehicle to pass
Option C: Brake suddenly to slow down the faster vehicle
Option D: Flash your lights to signal the faster vehicle to slow down

Question 29: What should you do if you are driving and come across an obstacle in the road?

Option A: Drive around the obstacle
Option B: Stop and wait for the obstacle to be removed
Option C: Drive over the obstacle
Option D: Turn around and find another route

Question 30: What is the maximum number of passengers allowed in a Class A vehicle in California?

Option A: 2
Option B: 4
Option C: 6
Option D: 8

Question 31: What should you do if you are driving and your engine begins to overheat?

Option A: Accelerate to reach your destination faster
Option B: Gradually reduce your speed and pull off the road
Option C: Ignore the overheating and continue driving
Option D: Turn off the air conditioning to reduce engine strain

Question 32: What should you do if you are driving on a road with a posted speed limit of 55 mph and the flow of traffic is moving faster?

Option A: Drive at the posted speed limit
Option B: Drive at the speed of the flow of traffic
Option C: Drive 10 mph over the posted speed limit
Option D: Turn around and find another route

Question 33: What should you do if you are driving and come across a road sign indicating a sharp turn ahead?

Option A: Slow down and take the turn at a moderate speed
Option B: Speed up to take the turn faster

Option C: Turn around and find another route
Option D: Drive straight through the turn

Question 34: What should you do if you are driving and your tires suddenly lose traction on a slippery road?

Option A: Apply the brakes suddenly
Option B: Turn the steering wheel in the opposite direction of the skid
Option C: Accelerate to try to regain control of the vehicle
Option D: Take your foot off the gas pedal and let the vehicle coast to a stop

Question 35: What should you do if you are driving and come across a road sign indicating a bridge ahead with a weight limit?

Option A: Drive across the bridge as quickly as possible
Option B: Turn around and find another route
Option C: Slow down and drive across the bridge with caution
Option D: Ignore the road sign and drive across the bridge normally

Question 36: What should you do when approaching a school bus with its stop arm extended?

Option A: Drive around the school bus
Option B: Stop and wait for the children to board or exit the bus
Option C: Slow down and proceed with caution
Option D: Honk your horn to signal the bus to move

1. Option A: Stop and look for pedestrians and traffic before proceeding
2. Option A: 25 mph
3. Option D: Anytime you're changing direction or moving in a different lane
4. Option B: Exchange information with the other driver and file a report with the DMV
5. Option C: 6
6. Option B: Slow down and move over to the lane farthest from the emergency vehicle
7. Option A: At any time
8. Option B: 55 mph
9. Option C: Call 911 and wait for medical and law enforcement assistance
10. Option B: 4
11. Option B: Come to a complete stop
12. Option A: You can proceed straight ahead or turn left
13. Option A: 20 mph
14. Option B: Call the police and wait for them to arrive
15. Option B: Pull over to the side of the road and wait for the rain to stop
16. Option B: Slow down and follow the posted speed limit in the construction zone
17. Option C: Move to the right lane if it is safe to do so
18. Option C: Slow down and be prepared to stop
19. Option B: Exchange information with the other driver and file a report with the DMV
20. Option C: Slow down and be prepared to stop
21. Option B: Honk to alert the driver his/her tail light is broken
22. Option B: Turn the steering wheel in the direction of the skid
23. Option C: Slow down and be prepared to stop

24. Option A: Use your turn signal
25. Option D: 8
26. Option A: Stop and wait for the vehicle to clear the intersection
27. Option C: Allow at least three feet of clearance when passing the bicycle
28. Option B: Move to the right lane to allow the faster vehicle to pass
29. Option B: Stop and look both ways before proceeding
30. Option D: 8
31. Option B: Gradually reduce your speed and pull off the road
32. Option A: Drive at the posted speed limit
33. Option A: Slow down and take the turn at a moderate speed
34. Option B: Turn the steering wheel in the opposite direction of the skid
35. Option C: Slow down and drive across the bridge with caution
36. Option B: Stop and wait for the children to board or exit the bus

PRACTICE TEST 5

Question 1: What should you do when you approach a steady green traffic light?

Option A: Stop and wait for the light to turn yellow
Option B: Proceed with caution and be prepared to stop if necessary
Option C: Drive through the intersection without slowing down
Option D: Honk your horn to clear the intersection

Question 2: When should you use your horn while driving?

Option A: When changing lanes
Option B: When passing other vehicles
Option C: To signal danger or frustration
Option D: Only in emergency situations

Question 3: What is the minimum speed limit on a two-lane rural highway in California?

Option A: 45 mph
Option B: 50 mph
Option C: 55 mph
Option D: 60 mph

Question 4: What should you do when approaching a vehicle that is parked along the side of the road?

Option A: Drive around the parked vehicle
Option B: Slow down and be prepared to stop
Option C: Drive through the parked vehicle
Option D: Honk your horn to signal the parked vehicle to move

Question 5: What should you do when approaching a curve in the road?

Option A: Drive through the curve as quickly as possible
Option B: Slow down and proceed with caution
Option C: Stop and wait for a clear view of the road
Option D: Yield to other vehicles in the area

Question 6: What should you do when approaching an intersection controlled by a stop sign?

Option A: Stop behind the white limit line
Option B: Slow down and proceed with caution
Option C: Drive through the intersection as quickly as possible
Option D: Yield to other vehicles and pedestrians in the area

Question 7: When driving in the left lane of a multi-lane highway, what should you do?

Option A: Drive as quickly as possible
Option B: Drive at a speed that is reasonable and prudent
Option C: Follow the speed of the slower vehicles in the right lane
Option D: Drive slower than the posted speed limit

Question 8: When is it safe to pass another vehicle?

Option A: When you're driving on a two-lane road
Option B: When you have a clear view of the road ahead
Option C: When there's no sign prohibiting passing
Option D: When the passing lane is clear of other vehicles and it is safe to do so

Question 9: What is the proper way to make a right turn at a red light?

Option A: Stop and then turn
Option B: Stop, check for pedestrians and then turn
Option C: Slow down and then turn
Option D: Slow down, check for pedestrians, and then turn

Question 10: What is the recommended following distance for vehicles traveling at 60 mph?

Option A: 2 seconds
Option B: 3 seconds
Option C: 4 seconds
Option D: 5 seconds

Question 11: When driving in fog, what should you use to increase your visibility?

Option A: High beams
Option B: Low beams
Option C: Hazard lights
Option D: No lights

Question 12: What should you do if you come to a roundabout and need to turn left?

Option A: Drive straight through the roundabout
Option B: Yield to traffic in the roundabout and turn left
Option C: Stop at the entrance of the roundabout
Option D: Turn around and find another route

Question 13: When entering a roundabout, which direction should you turn your wheels?

Option A: Left
Option B: Right
Option C: Straight
Option D: Toward the center of the roundabout

Question 14: What should you do if you are being tailgated by another vehicle?

Option A: Speed up to get away from the tailgater
Option B: Move to the right lane to let the tailgater pass
Option C: Brake suddenly to force the tailgater to back off
Option D: Increase your following distance to give the tailgater more room

Question 15: What should you do when you come to an uncontrolled T-intersection?

Option A: Stop and wait for other vehicles to clear
Option B: Slow down and proceed with caution
Option C: Yield to the vehicles on the road that you are entering
Option D: Drive through the intersection without slowing down

Question 16: What should you do when approaching a yield sign?

Option A: Stop and wait for traffic to clear
Option B: Slow down and proceed with caution
Option C: Stop and proceed when safe
Option D: Drive past the sign without slowing down

Question 17: When should you use your high beam headlights?

Option A: When following another vehicle closely
Option B: When driving on a rural road with no other vehicles around
Option C: When driving in fog or heavy rain
Option D: When approaching an intersection

Question 18: When entering an expressway, what lane should you be in?

Option A: The far-left lane
Option B: The far-right lane
Option C: Any lane, as long as it is safe
Option D: The center lane

Question 19: When approaching a roundabout, what should you do when yielding to pedestrians?

Option A: Stop and wait until they cross the entire roadway
Option B: Honk your horn to hurry them along
Option C: Proceed with caution, but do not come to a complete stop
Option D: Drive around the pedestrians, even if they are still crossing

Question 20: What should you do if you approach a green traffic light and there is a pedestrian crossing the street in a crosswalk

Option A: Drive through the intersection without slowing down
Option B: Stop and wait for the pedestrian to cross
Option C: Proceed with caution and yield to the pedestrian
Option D: Sound your horn to signal the pedestrian to cross

Question 21: What should you do when approaching a blind intersection?

Option A: Slow down and proceed with caution
Option B: Stop and proceed when safe
Option C: Drive past the intersection without slowing down
Option D: Sound your horn to signal your presence

Question 22: What should you do if you are involved in a collision with a parked vehicle and the owner is not present?

Option A: Leave a note with your contact information on the parked vehicle
Option B: Report the collision to the nearest police station
Option C: Drive away without leaving any information
Option D: Wait for the owner to return and provide your information

Question 23: When driving in California, what is the minimum insurance coverage required by law?

Option A: Liability coverage for property damage only
Option B: Liability coverage for bodily injury and property damage
Option C: Comprehensive coverage for both bodily injury and property damage
Option D: No insurance is required to drive in California.

Question 24: What is the proper hand signal for a lane change?

Option A: Right arm extended straight up in the air.
Option B: Left arm extended out of the window.
Option C: Right arm extended downward at a 90 degree angle.
Option D: Left arm extended horizontally.

Question 25: What should you do if you approach a vehicle with its four-way flashers on?

Option A: Speed up to get past the vehicle quickly.
Option B: Slow down and proceed with caution.
Option C: Stop and wait for the vehicle to move out of the road.
Option D: Honk your horn to signal your presence.

Question 26: What should you do when driving through a dust storm?

Option A: Speed up to get through it as fast as possible

Option B: Pull over to the side of the road and wait for it to pass
Option C: Drive with your hazard lights on
Option D: Keep driving normally, your car will protect you

Question 27: How should you signal when changing lanes on a freeway?

Option A: Use your hand signal
Option B: Use your emergency flashers
Option C: Use your turn signal
Option D: Wave to other drivers

Question 28: What should you do if you're driving and see an animal on the road ahead?

Option A: Swerve to avoid the animal, even if it means going into oncoming traffic
Option B: Honk your horn to scare the animal away
Option C: Slow down and proceed with caution
Option D: Keep driving at the same speed, the animal will move out of the way

Question 29: If you come to a stop sign and the crosswalk is painted on the road, where should you stop?

Option A: At the edge of the crosswalk before entering the intersection
Option B: In the middle of the crosswalk
Option C: Just before the stop sign
Option D: In the middle of the intersection

Question 30: If you come to a four-way stop and two cars arrive at the same time, who has the right of way?

Option A: The car on the right
Option B: The car on the left

Option C: The car going straight
Option D: The car making a left turn

Question 31: What should you do if you come across a horse and rider on the road?

Option A: Slow down and honk your horn.
Option B: Stop and wait for them to pass.
Option C: Speed up and pass them quickly.
Option D: Wave and shout to the horse.

Question 32: What should you do if you miss your exit on the freeway?

Option A: Stop on the shoulder and wait for help
Option B: Back up to the exit
Option C: Drive on the shoulder to reach the exit
Option D: Continue to the next exit and turn around

Question 33: What is the correct way to park on a hill with a curb?

Option A: Pointing uphill and close to the curb.
Option B: Pointing downhill and away from the curb.
Option C: Pointing downhill and close to the curb.
Option D: Pointing uphill and away from the curb.

Question 34: What should you do when you approach a flashing red traffic signal?

Option A: Stop, look both ways, and proceed with caution
Option B: Stop, then proceed when safe
Option C: Slow down and proceed with caution
Option D: Treat it as a stop sign

Question 35: What should you do if you're approaching a red light and the car in front of you suddenly stops?

Option A: Drive around the car, even if it means crossing a solid white line
Option B: Stop behind the car and wait for the light to change
Option C: Speed up and pass the car before the light changes
Option D: Honk your horn to get the car to move

Question 36: What should you do if you're approaching a green light and the car in front of you suddenly stops?

Option A: Drive around the car, even if it means crossing a solid white line
Option B: Stop behind the car and wait for it to proceed
Option C: Speed up and pass the car before the light changes
Option D: Honk your horn to get the car to move

PRACTICE TEST 5: ANSWERS

1. Option C: Drive through the intersection without slowing down
2. Option D: Only in emergency situations
3. Option B: 50 mph
4. Option B: Slow down and be prepared to stop
5. Option B: Slow down and proceed with caution
6. Option A: Stop behind the white limit line
7. Option B: Drive at a speed that is reasonable and prudent
8. Option D: When the passing lane is clear of other vehicles and it is safe to do so
9. Option B: Stop, check for pedestrians and then turn
10. Option B: 3 seconds
11. Option B: Low beams.
12. Option B: Yield to traffic in the roundabout and turn left
13. Option D: Toward the center of the roundabout.
14. Option D: Increase your following distance to give the tailgater more room
15. Option C: Yield to the vehicles on the road that you are entering.
16. Option B: Slow down and proceed with caution
17. Option B: When driving on a rural road with no other vehicles around.
18. Option A: The far-left lane.
19. Option C: Proceed with caution, but do not come to a complete stop
20. Option B: Stop and wait for the pedestrian to cross
21. Option A: Slow down and proceed with caution
22. Option A: Leave a note with your contact information on the parked vehicle
23. Option B: Liability coverage for bodily injury and property damage.
24. Option D: Left arm extended horizontally.
25. Option B: Slow down and proceed with caution.

26. Option B: Pull over to the side of the road and wait for it to pass.
27. Option C: Use your turn signal
28. Option C: Slow down and proceed with caution.
29. Option A: At the edge of the crosswalk before entering the intersection.
30. Option A: The car on the right. When two cars arrive at a four-way stop at the same time, the car on the right should go first.
31. Option B: Stop and wait for them to pass.
32. Option D: Continue to the next exit and turn around
33. Option C: Pointing downhill and close to the curb.
34. Option A: Stop, look both ways, and proceed with caution
35. Option B: Stop behind the car and wait for the light to change
36. Option B: Stop behind the car and wait for it to proceed

PRACTICE TEST 6

Question 1: What should you do if you're driving on a highway and come across a toll booth?

Option A: Keep driving, the toll booth is only for slower vehicles
Option B: Slow down and pay the toll fee
Option C: Honk your horn to signal the toll collector to open the gate
Option D: Drive around the toll booth, there's no need to stop

Question 2: What should you do when approaching a yellow diamond-shaped sign with a black X?

Option A: Slow down, the road ahead is closed
Option B: Drive through the sign, there's no need to stop
Option C: Stop and wait for further instructions
Option D: Speed up and get through the area as quickly as possible

Question 3: When driving in fog, what should you use to help you see the road ahead?

Option A: High beams
Option B: Low beams
Option C: Parking lights
Option D: Hazard lights

Question 4: What should you do when approaching a roundabout with a flashing yellow arrow pointing to the left?

Option A: Yield to vehicles already in the roundabout and enter when there is a gap
Option B: Drive as fast as possible through the roundabout
Option C: Turn left without yielding to oncoming traffic

Option D: Stop and wait for the arrow to turn green before entering the roundabout

Question 5: What should you do if you see a deer on the road ahead?

Option A: Swerve to avoid hitting the deer
Option B: Brake hard to stop before hitting the deer
Option C: Honk your horn to scare the deer away
Option D: Increase your speed to get through the area quickly

Question 6: What should you do if you see a pedestrian using a white cane or guide dog?

Option A: Yield the right-of-way and proceed with caution
Option B: Honk your horn and proceed
Option C: Speed up to get around the pedestrian
Option D: Swerve around the pedestrian into the other lane

Question 7: What should you do when approaching a flashing green traffic signal?

Option A: Stop and wait for the signal to turn red
Option B: Slow down and proceed with caution
Option C: Proceed with normal speed
Option D: Make a U-turn if safe

Question 8: When driving in heavy rain, what should you do to increase visibility and avoid hydroplaning?

Option A: Drive faster to get through the rain more quickly
Option B: Use your high beams to see better
Option C: Reduce your speed and increase your following distance
Option D: Drive in the center lane to avoid water puddles

Question 9: What should you do when driving in a roundabout?

Option A: Stop at the entrance and wait for traffic to clear.
Option B: Drive on the shoulder to bypass the roundabout.
Option C: Yield to traffic already in the roundabout.
Option D: Honk your horn to warn other drivers.

Question 10: What is the minimum passing distance required by law when passing a bicycle on the road in California?

Option A: Three feet
Option B: Four feet
Option C: Five feet
Option D: Six feet

Question 11: What should you do if a traffic signal light is not working?

Option A: Treat the intersection as a four-way stop.
Option B: Treat the intersection as if the light were green.
Option C: Wait for other drivers to indicate which way to proceed.
Option D: Treat the intersection as if the light were flashing yellow

Question 12: What should you do when you are merging onto a highway from an entrance ramp?

Option A: Slow down and wait for a gap in traffic.
Option B: Speed up and force your way into traffic.
Option C: Drive on the shoulder until you can merge safely.
Option D: Stop on the entrance ramp and wait for traffic to clear

Question 13: What should you do when you approach a green arrow signal that is about to turn yellow?

Option A: Stop immediately
Option B: Speed up to get through the intersection before the light turns red
Option C: Proceed with caution, but do not stop
Option D: Stop if necessary, but proceed if you can safely do so

Question 14: What should you do when driving in a tunnel with low visibility?

Option A: Use your high beams to see better
Option B: Use your parking lights to be more visible to other drivers
Option C: Slow down and increase your following distance
Option D: Drive in the center lane to avoid water puddles

Question 15: What is the minimum passing distance required by law when passing a vehicle that is stopped at a crosswalk in California?

Option A: Three feet
Option B: Four feet
Option C: Five feet
Option D: Six feet

Question 16: What is the maximum number of passengers allowed in a car with only one seatbelt in California?

Option A: 3
Option B: 4
Option C: 5
Option D: 6

Question 17: What is the minimum fine for a person caught driving under the influence of drugs or alcohol in California?

Option A: $1000

Option B: $1500
Option C: $2000
Option D: $2500

Question 18: When merging onto a freeway, what should you do?

Option A: Signal and gradually accelerate to match the speed of the traffic on the freeway.
Option B: Stop at the end of the ramp and wait for a gap in traffic.
Option C: Drive onto the shoulder and wait for a gap in traffic.
Option D: Drive onto the freeway at a high speed and force your way into traffic.

Question 19: What is the maximum number of hours a person can drive consecutively in California without taking a break?

Option A: 5 hours
Option B: 6 hours
Option C: 7 hours
Option D: 8 hours

Question 20: What is the fine for driving without proof of insurance in California?

Option A: $100
Option B: $250
Option C: $500
Option D: $1000

Question 21: What is the California "Three Feet for Safety" law used for?

Option A: To ensure a safe following distance while driving
Option B: To regulate the use of high beam headlights

Option C: To enforce the use of seat belts
Option D: To prohibit the use of cell phones while driving

Question 22: What is the fine for running a red light in California?

Option A: $100
Option B: $150
Option C: $200
Option D: $250

Question 23: What should you do when a road is completely covered in ice?

Option A: Stop and wait until the ice melts
Option B: Drive slowly and carefully, maintaining control of your vehicle
Option C: Speed up to get through the ice quickly
Option D: Get out and walk on the ice to test its thickness

Question 24: What should you do if a bee flies into your car while you're driving?

Option A: Swat at the bee and risk losing control of your vehicle
Option B: Stop the car immediately and exit to remove the bee
Option C: Ignore the bee and continue driving as usual
Option D: Roll down the windows and continue driving as usual

Question 25: What should you do if you approach a pedestrian who is crossing the street illegally?

Option A: Blast your horn to warn them to get out of the way
Option B: Slow down and be prepared to stop
Option C: Drive around the pedestrian, even if it means going into the sidewalk
Option D: Speed up to get past the pedestrian before they cross

Question 26: When should you use your turn signals while driving?

Option A: Only when driving in busy traffic.
Option B: Only when changing lanes or turning.
Option C: Only when you see other drivers using their turn signals.
Option D: Anytime you change lanes, turn, or merge.

Question 27: What should you do if you see a horse and rider on the road ahead?

Option A: Stop and wait for them to pass
Option B: Honk your horn to scare the horse
Option C: Drive around them on the shoulder of the road
Option D: Speed up and pass them as quickly as possible

Question 28: What should you do if you get lost while driving?
Option A: Keep driving in the same direction
Option B: Ask for directions from a passerby
Option C: Pull over and look at a map or GPS
Option D: Make sudden and unpredictable turns

Question 29: What should you do when driving in the mountains?

Option A: Increase your speed to get up the mountain faster.
Option B: Decrease your speed and allow for longer stopping distances.
Option C: Drive at the same speed as you would on flat roads.
Option D: Drive on the shoulder of the road to get around slow vehicles.

Question 30: What should you do if you are driving in a car with a manual transmission and the engine stalls?

Option A: Shift into neutral and restart the engine.
Option B: Shift into park and restart the engine.
Option C: Leave the vehicle in gear and try to restart the engine.
Option D: Shift into reverse and restart the engine.

Question 31: What is the correct hand signal for a stop?

Option A: Extend your arm straight out to the right
Option B: Extend your arm straight out to the left
Option C: Bend your arm at the elbow and point downwards
Option D: Wave your arm back and forth

Question 32: What should you do if you are merging onto a highway and a car is already in the lane that you want to enter?

Option A: Speed up to get in front of the other car
Option B: Slow down and let the other car merge first
Option C: Stop on the ramp and wait for a break in traffic
Option D: Force your way into the lane

Question 33: What is the maximum speed limit on an undivided two-lane road?

Option A: 55 mph
Option B: 60 mph
Option C: 65 mph
Option D: 70 mph

Question 34: What should you do if you are driving and suddenly your steering wheel locks?

Option A: Panic and try to jerk the wheel to get it to turn
Option B: Apply the brakes and pull over to the side of the road
Option C: Keep driving straight ahead
Option D: Accelerate to try and break the lock

Question 35: What is the minimum speed limit on a freeway?

Option A: 50 mph
Option B: 55 mph
Option C: 60 mph
Option D: 65 mph

Question 36: When can you legally park in a crosswalk?

Option A: Anytime, as long as you don't obstruct pedestrian traffic.
Option B: Never, crosswalks are always off-limits for parking.
Option C: During rush hour, when there is less pedestrian traffic.
Option D: Only when there is no pedestrian traffic and you have the right of way.

PRACTICE TEST 6: ANSWERS

1. Option B: Slow down and pay the toll fee
2. Option A: Slow down, the road ahead is closed
3. Option B: Low beams
4. Option A: Yield to vehicles already in the roundabout and enter when there is a gap
5. Option B: Brake hard to stop before hitting the deer
6. Option A: Yield the right-of-way and proceed with caution
7. Option C: Proceed with normal speed
8. Option C: Reduce your speed and increase your following distance
9. Option C: Yield to traffic already in the roundabout.
10. Option A: Three feet
11. Option A: Treat the intersection as a four-way stop.
12. Option A: Slow down and wait for a gap in traffic.
13. Option D: Stop if necessary, but proceed if you can safely do so
14. Option C: Slow down and increase your following distance
15. Option A: Three feet
16. Option B: 4
17. Option B: $1500
18. Option A: Signal and gradually accelerate to match the speed of the traffic on the freeway.
19. Option D: 8 hours
20. Option C: $500.
21. Option A: The California "Three Feet for Safety" law is used to ensure a safe following distance while driving.
22. Option B: The fine for running a red light in California is $150.
23. Option B: Drive slowly and carefully, maintaining control of your vehicle.
24. Option D: Roll down the windows and continue driving as usual
25. Option B Slow down and be prepared to stop.

26. Option D: Anytime you change lanes, turn, or merge.
27. Option A: Stop and wait for them to pass
28. Option C: Pull over and look at a map or GPS
29. Option B: Decrease your speed and allow for longer stopping distances.
30. Option A: Shift into neutral and restart the engine.
31. Option C: Bend your arm at the elbow and point downwards
32. Option B: Slow down and let the other car merge first
33. Option A: 55 mph
34. Option B: Apply the brakes and pull over to the side of the road
35. Option B: 55 mph
36. Option B: Never, crosswalks are always off-limits for parking.

PRACTICE TEST 7

Question 1: What is the maximum speed limit in a business district?

Option A: 35 mph
Option B: 40 mph
Option C: 25 mph
Option D: 30 mph

Question 2: What is the minimum speed limit on a multi-lane freeway?

Option A: 45 mph
Option B: 50 mph
Option C: 55 mph
Option D: 60 mph

Question 3: What should you do when driving in a construction zone?

Option A: Slow down and be prepared for changes in traffic patterns.
Option B: Speed up to get through the construction zone as quickly as possible.
Option C: Ignore any traffic control devices or signs in the construction zone.
Option D: Drive on the shoulder of the road to bypass the construction zone.

Question 4: What should you do if you are driving and see a tornado approaching?

Option A: Stop your car and hide under an overpass
Option B: Drive towards the tornado to get a better look

Option C: Continue driving at a normal speed
Option D: Pull over and get out of the car

Question 5: What should you do if you are driving and a child runs into the street?

Option A: Brake suddenly and swerve to avoid the child.
Option B: Honk your horn to warn the child.
Option C: Increase your speed to get around the child.
Option D: Slow down or stop, and be prepared to take evasive action if necessary.

Question 6: How often should you rotate your tires?

Option A: Every 6 months
Option B: Every time you change the oil
Option C: Every 10,000 miles
Option D: Every 2 years

Question 7: What is the correct hand signal for a right turn?

Option A: Bend your arm at the elbow and point downwards
Option B: Wave your arm back and forth
Option C: Bend your arm at the elbow and point upwards
Option D: Extend your arm straight out to the left

Question 8: What is the minimum speed limit on a multi-lane freeway?

Option A: 45 mph
Option B: 50 mph
Option C: 55 mph
Option D: 60 mph

Question 9: What should you do if you are driving in dense fog and your visibility is severely limited?

Option A: Turn on your high beams to see better
Option B: Slow down and pull over to the side of the road until visibility improves
Option C: Speed up to get through the fog more quickly
Option D: Keep driving at the same speed you were before

Question 10: What is the maximum speed limit on a rural two-lane road?

Option A: 55 mph
Option B: 60 mph
Option C: 65 mph
Option D: 70 mph

Question 11: What is the maximum speed limit in a business district?

Option A: 25 mph
Option B: 30 mph
Option C: 35 mph
Option D: 40 mph

Question 12: What is the maximum speed limit in a residential area at night?

Option A: 20 mph
Option B: 25 mph
Option C: 30 mph
Option D: 35 mph

Question 13: What is the minimum distance a driver should keep when following a motorcycle in California?

Option A: One Car Length
Option B: Two Motorcycle Lengths

Option C: Three Car Lengths
Option D: Half a Car Length

Question 14: What should a driver do when approaching a crosswalk with a blind pedestrian using a cane?

Option A: Slow down and be prepared to stop
Option B: Honk the horn
Option C: Speed up and pass the pedestrian quickly
Option D: Yell at the pedestrian to get out of the way

Question 15: What should you do when driving in a residential area?

Option A: Drive at a speed that is appropriate for the conditions.
Option B: Drive as quickly as possible to reach your destination.
Option C: Drive on the sidewalk to avoid congestion on the road
Option D: Drive on the wrong side of the road to get around slow-moving vehicles.

Question 16: What should you do if you are approaching a railroad crossing with no warning signals and no gates?

Option A: Stop before the tracks and look both ways
Option B: Slow down and proceed with caution
Option C: Speed up to get across the tracks quickly
Option D: Drive around the crossing

Question 17: What should you do if you encounter a roundabout?

Option A: Drive straight through the roundabout without stopping
Option B: Yield to drivers already in the roundabout
Option C: Stop at the entrance to the roundabout and wait for a gap in traffic

Option D: Sound your horn to signal other drivers

Question 18: What should you do when approaching a steep downhill road?

Option A: Shift into a lower gear and drive slowly.
Option B: Maintain your current speed to conserve momentum.
Option C: Increase your speed to get down the hill more quickly.
Option D: Drive on the shoulder of the road to avoid the steep slope.

Question 19: What should you do when driving on a highway with multiple lanes in the same direction?

Option A: Drive in the right lane unless passing.
Option B: Drive in the left lane as much as possible.
Option C: Drive in the middle lane to avoid traffic in the other lanes.
Option D: Drive in any lane you prefer.

Question 20: What should you do when driving behind a low-moving vehicle travelling under the minimum speed limit on a two-lane road?

Option A: Pass the vehicle on the left when it is safe to do so.
Option B: Follow the slow-moving vehicle closely.
Option C: Drive on the shoulder of the road to get around the low-moving vehicle.
Option D: Honk your horn to signal the slow-moving vehicle to speed up.

Question 21: What is the maximum speed limit in a school zone during school hours?

Option A: 25 mph
Option B: 30 mph

Option C: 35 mph
Option D: 40 mph

Question 22: What should you do if you approach a vehicle that is merging into your lane?

Option A: Speed up to prevent the vehicle from merging
Option B: Slow down or change lanes to let the vehicle merge
Option C: Sound your horn to get the vehicle to move faster
Option D: Drive as close as possible to the merging vehicle to prevent it from merging

Question 23: What is the minimum speed limit on a scenic highway?

Option A: 30 mph
Option B: 35 mph
Option C: 40 mph
Option D: 45 mph

Question 24: What should you do when driving on a road with a solid double yellow line in the center?

Option A: Pass other vehicles when it is safe to do so.
Option B: Drive on the shoulder of the road to avoid the solid double yellow line.
Option C: Follow other vehicles closely.
Option D: Cross the solid double yellow line to pass other vehicles when it is safe to do so.

Question 25: When driving in a construction zone, what should you do if you see a flagger directing traffic?

Option A: Ignore the flagger and proceed through the construction zone as normal.
Option B: Slow down and follow the flagger's directions.

Option C: Speed up to get through the construction zone quickly.
Option D: Honk your horn to alert the flagger.

Question 26: What should you do if you encounter a pedestrian crossing the road at a crosswalk?

Option A: Drive as close as possible to the pedestrian to scare them
Option B: Honk your horn to warn the pedestrian
Option C: Slow down and allow the pedestrian to cross
Option D: Drive around the pedestrian on the shoulder of the road

Question 27: When driving on a two-way road with one lane in each direction, what should you do if a vehicle is passing you on the left?

Option A: Speed up to prevent the passing vehicle from passing you.
Option B: Move to the right and allow the passing vehicle to pass safely.
Option C: Brake suddenly to slow down the passing vehicle.
Option D: Turn into the passing vehicle's lane to block it from passing.

Question 28: What should you do when driving on a road with a solid white line on your side?

Option A: Follow other vehicles closely.
Option B: Drive on the shoulder of the road to avoid the solid white line.
Option C: Cross the solid white line to pass other vehicles when is safe to do so.
Option D: Stay within the boundaries of the solid white line.

Question 29: When driving in the left lane on a multi-lane road, what is the maximum speed limit you can legally drive?

Option A: 50 mph
Option B: 55 mph
Option C: 60 mph
Option D: 65 mph

Question 30: When driving in a tunnel, what should you do if the car in front of you has its headlights on?

Option A: Turn off your headlights.
Option B: Increase your following distance.
Option C: Decrease your following distance.
Option D: Keep your headlights on.

Question 31: What should you do if you are driving on a road with a 35 mph speed limit and come across a blind pedestrian with a guide dog?

Option A: Slow down and proceed with caution.
Option B: Honk your horn to alert the pedestrian.
Option C: Stop and wait for the pedestrian to cross the road.
Option D: Drive around the pedestrian quickly.

Question 32: When is it legal to park your vehicle on the side of a highway?

Option A: During the day.
Option B: At night.
Option C: When it's raining.
Option D: When it's not allowed by any signs or pavement markings.

Question 33: What should you do if you are driving on a two-lane road and see a car approaching from the opposite direction with its high beams on?

Option A: Flash your high beams at the oncoming vehicle
Option B: Look at the right edge of the road
Option C: Look directly at the oncoming vehicle's lights
Option D: Slow down and proceed with caution

Question 34: What should you do if you approach a road sign that is partially obscured by tree branches?

Option A: Ignore the sign
Option B: Slow down and proceed with caution
Option C: Speed up to get past the sign quickly
Option D: Stop and wait for the road sign to become clear

Question 35: What should you do if you encounter a vehicle with its hazard lights flashing on the side of the road?

Option A: Drive past the vehicle as quickly as possible
Option B: Slow down and proceed with caution
Option C: Stop and wait for the vehicle to move
Option D: Drive around the vehicle on the shoulder of the road

Question 36: What is the correct hand signal for slowing down or stopping?

Option A: Bend your arm at the elbow and point downwards
Option B: Wave your arm back and forth
Option C: Extend your arm straight out to the left
Option D: Bend your arm at the elbow and point upwards

PRACTICE TEST 7: ANSWERS

1. Option A: 35 mph
2. Option A: 45 mph
3. Option A: Slow down and be prepared for changes in traffic patterns.
4. Option D: Pull over and get out of the car
5. Option D: Slow down or stop, and be prepared to take evasive action if necessary.
6. Option C: Every 10,000 miles
7. Option C: Bend your arm at the elbow and point upwards
8. Option A: 45 mph
9. Option B: Slow down and pull over to the side of the road until visibility improves
10. Option B: 60 mph
11. Option A: 25 mph
12. Option B: 25 mph
13. Option B: Two Motorcycle Lengths
14. Option A: Slow down and be prepared to stop
15. Option A: Drive at a speed that is appropriate for the conditions.
16. Option A: Stop before the tracks and look both ways
17. Option B: Yield to drivers already in the roundabout
18. Option A: Shift into a lower gear and drive slowly.
19. Option A: Drive in the right lane unless passing.
20. Option A: Pass the vehicle on the left when it is safe to do so.
21. Option A: 25 mph
22. Option B: Slow down or change lanes to let the vehicle merge
23. Option A: 30 mph
24. Option D: Cross the solid double yellow line to pass other vehicles when it is safe to do so.
25. Option B: Slow down and follow the flagger's directions.
26. Option C: Slow down and allow the pedestrian to cross

27. Option B: Move to the right and allow the passing vehicle to pass safely.
28. Option D: Stay within the boundaries of the solid white line.
29. Option D: 65 mph
30. Option B: Increase your following distance.
31. Option C: Stop and wait for the pedestrian to cross the road.
32. Option D: When it's not allowed by any signs or pavement markings.
33. Option B: Look at the right edge of the road
34. Option B: Slow down and proceed with caution
35. Option B: Slow down and proceed with caution
36. Option A: Bend your arm at the elbow and point downwards

Made in the USA
Las Vegas, NV
24 January 2024